SEA PLANTS

THE SEA

Jason Cooper

The Rourke Corporation, Inc.
Vero Beach, Florida 32964

Edited by Sandra A. Robinson

PHOTO CREDITS
All photos © Lynn M. Stone; illustration, page 7, © C. Allen Elsbree

LIBRARY OF CONGRESS
Library of Congress Cataloging-in-Publication Data
Cooper, Jason, 1942-
    Sea plants / by Jason Cooper.
    p. cm. — (Discovery library of the sea)
    Includes index.
    Summary: Describes some of the plants found in the oceans, in
salt marshes, and along the seashore and their importance to the
ecology.
    ISBN 0-86593-232-8
    1. Marine flora—Juvenile literature. 2. Marine ecology—Juvenile
literature. [1. Marine plants. 2. Marine ecology. 3. Ecology.] I. Title.
II. Series: Cooper, Jason, 1942-   Discovery library of the sea.
QK931.C66 1992
581.92—dc20   92-16076
                                         CIP
                                         AC

TABLE OF CONTENTS

SEA PLANTS

The sea is the world's largest garden. Like any other garden—a field of corn or a forest of trees—the sea is a nursery for plants.

Sea plants make it possible for sea, or **marine,** animals to exist. All marine animals—oysters, shrimp, fish, whales and others—depend upon plants in one way or another for their survival.

Green algae plants grow along the rocky Maine coast

PLANKTON

"Plankton" is the name for billions of tiny ocean plants, animals and plantlike **organisms.**

Some types of plankton are barely visible. Others are **microscopic.** They are so small that they can be seen only under the powerful lens of a microscope.

The organisms, or living things, that make up plankton drift in the oceans. Some parts of the oceans are richer in plankton than others.

Plankton is extremely important. It forms the basic food of the sea.

Artist's drawing of microscopic diatom, one of the most important plankton plants (shown many times larger than life)

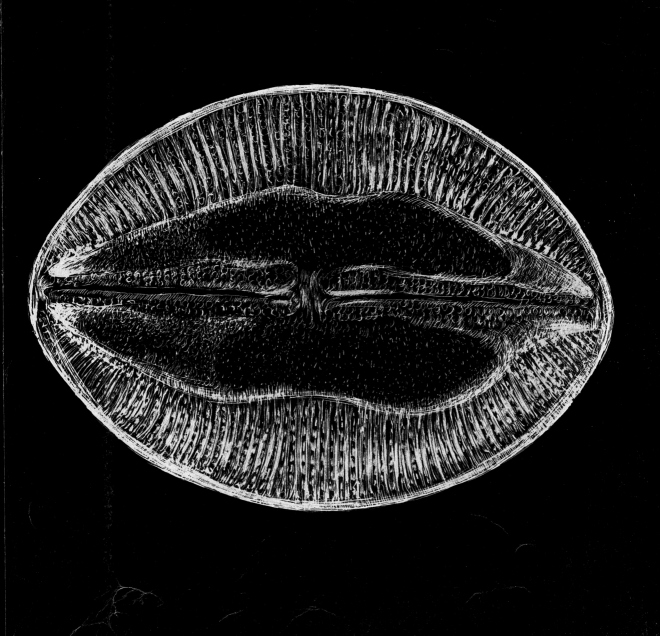

PLANTS AS FOOD

Sea plants feed the animals of the ocean. Plants become part of a food chain. They are passed from one link in the chain—an animal—to another.

For example, a small fish lives on a diet of plankton plants. A larger fish catches and eats the small fish. In turn, a hungry porpoise or pelican eats, or **preys** upon, the larger fish.

Neither the porpoise nor pelican eats plants. But without plant life, there would not be a small fish to feed the large fish to feed the pelican and porpoise!

Brown pelican gobbles a small fish that grew by eating plankton

SEAWEEDS

The best-known marine plants are seaweeds. Several **species,** or kinds, of seaweed grow in the sea.

Seaweeds belong to the **algae** family. These plants have no flowers, and many of them are brown, yellow, white or pink instead of green.

Seaweeds have many curious names that help explain what they look or feel like: cup and saucer, sea cauliflower, sea lettuce, sea sac, sea tar, crisp leather, sea brush and coral seaweed.

Pink coral seaweed shares Oregon ocean bottom with green algae and purple sea urchins

Sea oats help anchor beaches against high waves

Surfgrass grows in a Pacific tide pool

GIANT SEAWEED

Imagine a "ribbon" of giant seaweed that can reach from one end of a football field to the other.

Some of the giant brown seaweeds, known as kelp, grow in tangled, undersea forests along the coasts of southern California and western Mexico. Sea otters nap in floating kelp and hunt among its underwater leaves.

Giant kelp is one of the seaweeds used in food products for people.

A California sea otter wraps itself in floating kelp

LAWNS OF THE SEA

Sea grasses form great, green lawns in shallow sea water and along some seashores.

Many marine animals, such as sea urchins, sea trout, crabs and snails, live among the sea grasses. Sea grasses are also a favorite food of certain geese and green sea turtles.

In some patches of sea grass, each blade of grass is crusty with tiny sea animals.

A lawn of undersea turtle grass in the Gulf of Mexico

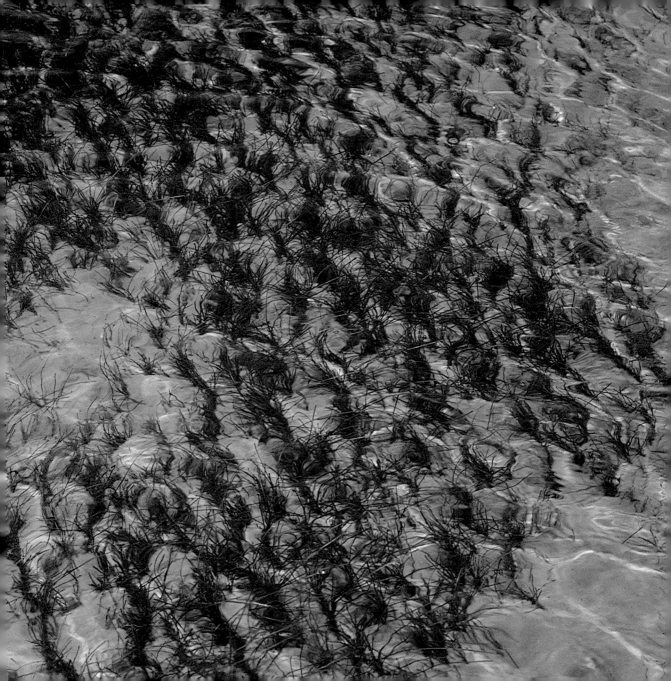

SALT MARSH PLANTS

Along some seashores, rivers and streams of seawater reach from the ocean into low-lying lands. Many kinds of grasses and grasslike plants grow in these muddy, wet lands, called salt marshes.

The roots of salt marsh plants help anchor the land so that it isn't washed away by waves during storms.

When salt marsh plants die, they rot, or **decay,** into tiny plant particles. The particles are food for little marine animals.

Salt marshes produce such creatures as oysters, crabs, clams, shrimps and many kinds of fish.

Salt marshes are homes for a variety of marine animals

TREES THAT STAND IN THE SEA

There is nothing ordinary about mangrove trees. They are the only North American trees that grow in seawater.

The red mangrove is easy to recognize. Its trunk stands on a web of spidery roots in shallow ocean bays.

The decaying leaves and twigs of mangroves fall into the sea and feed marine animals.

In the United States, mangrove forests grow only along the muddy seashores of southern Florida.

Red mangroves stand on curious, stiltlike roots in a shallow Florida bay

BEACH PLANTS

Beach plants are not true sea plants because they do not live in seawater. But they live on seashores, and they have to resist salty wind and ocean spray. The roots of beach plants grow in sandy, salty soil that would kill most plants.

The roots of such beach plants as sea oats, beach plum, tree lupine, morning-glories and sea grape are important to the seashore. Their roots help keep the soil from being washed into the sea.

Glossary

algae (AL jee) — a group of nonflowering plants, many of which are seaweeds and live in salt water

decay (deh KAY) — to rot; the process by which once living organisms are broken down into tiny particles

marine (muh REEN) — of or relating to the sea, salt water

microscopic (my kro SCAHP ik) — able to be seen only through the powerful lens of a microscope

organism (OR gan izm) — a living thing

prey (PRAY) — to hunt another animal for food; an animal that is hunted by another for food

species (SPEE sheez) — within a group of closely related plants, such as mangroves, one certain kind or type (*red* mangrove)

INDEX